# Reading Leaves

## Selected Poems

by

Bryan Ness

Nessessary Productions, 46 Mobile Manor, Angwin, CA 94508
©2012 by Bryan Ness & Nessessary Productions

Printed in the United States of America

Some of these poems originally appeared in the following periodicals:
*Ebbing Tide, Joey & the Black Boots, The Lamp-Post, Manna, Muse of Fire, Poetalk, Quicksilver, Romeo's Barking Machine, Spectrum, Spectrum's Edge, Tooth and Claw.*

Cover art by Bryan Ness.

ISBN-10: 0615685366
ISBN-13: 978-0615685366

*To my sister, Karen,*
*who is safely in God's hands*

# Table of Contents

## FIRST PAGE

A blank page to be filled
And more to follow.
What gets put there could
Be left to chance,
Or planned precisely
Without a misplaced syllable,
With each image and simile
Laid out in patient rows
Like Flander's Field,
Its granite slabs, row on row.

Both are faults committed
By printer's press
Or bleeding, writer's pen,
And books are only written well
Like sandpipers weaving skillfully
Between the land and sea,
Pausing only long enough
To probe the sand for food
And then it's off to dodge another surge.

READING LEAVES

Sifting through the leaves
grounded to be ground tomorrow
finding a few to immortalize on paper
chosen for their special curves or symmetry or
maybe because at 7 or 8
I found a leaf of just the same color
blended red and yellow with
just a memory of green
after being sucked of chlorophyll
saved for next year's foliage.
Under these same backyard trees
plums and wormy apples,
piled among the leaves to rot,
left purple stains on our
back porch steps and kitchen linoleum.
My father never raked them
into piles like in stories I read but
left them where they fell to
gradually blacken in the rain
yellowing the grass hidden
waiting for spring when transformations
meet the need for color.
Standing ankle-deep today in oak leaves—
neither plum nor apple—
still the shapes and colors
by some strange internal alteration
look the same, untouched by rain and
thirty years of practice.

## AGATE HUNTING

We walk along the pebble-piled beach
beside the murmur of the falling tide.

The slanting rays of afternoon reflect
and turn the stones and water into stars,

all alike to me. I bend and sift
coming up with nothing more than quartz,

distracted by the shiny water covered
rocks that keep my eyes from seeing agates.

You upon your own starry track
with better-trained eyes discover jewels

I have missed. You find ten to every
hard won agate left for me to find.

Your eye somehow grades the glint by shades
I never see, by practiced skills rehearsed

in childhood, walking the beach beside your dad,
his eye better then, he challenged you

by his skill. You strained to find just one
more agate, somehow always a couple short.

## Duke University Chapel

Inside these walls and roof of stone and glass
The light is split and broken, shattered it passes
Through my skin and flesh. I breathe the past
And present concurrently with the masses
Kneeling by these wooden benches filled
With more than light. The organ swells its song,
The sound reviving stone the workmen stilled
So long ago (their curves were cut so strong
Their edges speak). These pillars reach above
Like Adam at his birth, and as I stare
I touch the naked hand of yearning love
Between the stony heart and God's despair:
As Adam's promised seed breathes His last
The music dies, the echoes having passed.

## WOODS REQUIEM

They cut our woods and all that's left is dirt
Between the larger trees, untouched dessert
Left standing for another meal. It took
A week to clear and burn the weathered book
That took a hundred years to write in ink
Of chlorophyll and tannin. Now our link
With nature's past is just a few old leaves
whose tattered edges tell of past reprieves.
It will grow back as woods have always done
But how many years before they look as filled
With life as they did a week ago? The sun
Will do its work along with rain that's spilled
From winter skies, And only those who've stood
Among those trees will miss the former wood.

FIVE NOCTURNES

I

Coyote barks and howls wake up the moon
who runs his fingers through the trees (like harp
strings plucked), arpeggios settle to the ground
and silver fragments scatter through my window.

II

Moon-set happened hours ago.
The woods are dark with shades of black,
and all I sense are sounds: The wind
and tree tops lost in conversation,
between the surge of voices, drops,
condensing from the fog, let loose
from leaves above and flatten with
a chorus of pops, and somewhere branches
snap from passing feet and fur.

III

The snow is falling, and though it's night
the whiteness glows, like paper ash
blown up the flue that settles on
the ground, but more diffuse, as if
the light of a thousand coldly burning
stars were rolled out flat.

IV

The rhythm of the waves upon this shore,
unbroken breakers, mark out time in grains
of sand produced or tossed between the line
of land and ocean. Fog blocks out the light
of stars and moon and makes reality
composed of sound. A foghorn sings the bass,
waves percussion, to the melody
of bells from distant buoys; The mixing of
the ancient song with modern counterpoint.

V

Standing on a boat at night,
the waning moon above,
the ocean lives and breathes.
A hundred thousand fish or more slide past
and light the ocean's tiny fires,
their glowing embers dance the waves;
a seal glides below the swarm
and hurls it skyward with a brilliant flash.

## CHEMICAL BEING

Carbon, Hydrogen, Oxygen—
Covalent bonding in isomers arranged—
Electronegativity in
An aqueous organic soup,
Held in shape and molar state
By myriad hydrogen bonds. My
Hand is poised above the page
Glucose is transformed by
Oxygen to water and wasted $CO_2$;
Membranes come to life
And ions redistribute as
electric currents surge.
Muscle proteins in response,
Tighten, tense,
Strain against the bone,
and fingers move,
Pencil scrapes
Across the paperscape
Leaving carbon stains,
A symbol of the chemistry
Of brain and arm,
Bone and muscle;
A reinterpretation of
The complex brew of being.

INTERPRETATION

Crawling toward the sun
Reptile skin shimmering,
Eyes darting, head
Swaying side to side,
Wary predator,
Accidental prey,
A shadow moves, muscles
Tense to spring or fly
The size is so important
Since mistakes regretted
Are more than old shed skins
Drying in the sun
Below a favored perch.
So much depends upon
Correct interpretation
Of sunlight, shadow, sound,
And subtle sense of smell,
A spider's web, a knife
Edge, divide the night
From day, life from death.
Judging the shadow right
Insect exoskeleton
Hiding softer flesh
Is broken and transformed
To lizard flesh and bone.

JOSHUA TREE

Arms sprawled in semaphore,
Message signaled patiently by
Years of dry, dead sheaths,

You speak a harsh language
In an even harsher land
Where frost upon the brow
Meets naked sun and wind
Not bitter cold but dry.

And yet you find in this
Precarious soul of yours to
Paint your flowers white to
Atone for desert waste.

## WHITE ON WHITE

All I see is white:
the ground is white,
the trees are white,
the sky is white,
and one black cat
paints his way across the hill
leaving only white on white.

AT A LOSS FOR WORDS

Pen and pencil desecrate
the finely printed page
attempting (tempting?) wisdom,
at least to show in part
a knowledge gained
by hours of ATP consumed
in sleepless funneling
of pictures, words, diagrams
into neural circuitry
enhancing recall of fact
or more than fact, of synergy,
of layered fact on fact
connected fact to fact
to form a discipline.
Oblivion nestles close
as reconstruction falters,
hands go cold from loss of blood,
a fog obscures the map,
and wandering blind in fear,
approaching darkness, paralyzed
before the fall, a bitter taste
of rust in premonition bathes
the dying tongue.
Familiar objects turn into ghosts
who whisper cryptically,
time distorts
so seconds equal minutes, minutes seconds
and death is slowed for lack of time.

## GRANDPA'S CLAW

One arm, and one bright, shiny hook
he used like a crab claw,
his shirt a blade of tattered kelp,
he stitched the gape with mother of pearl
in every button hole,
his claw flashing and clicking.

At eleven I never thought to ask
the reason for the claw;
it worked so well
and it was all I ever knew of him.
my mother taught me not to ask,
and both my hands
had always been deformed.

I thought he too was born that way,
but learned years later
that accidents can happen too;
that machines, like people,
can remove an arm and sometimes more.

# A History of the Edge

Exploring the world is dangerous
no matter who you are.

Before Columbus many feared
the edge. One moment the sea
is smooth and slow, then
the current, pulled by gravity,
begins to speed toward the edge.
Your last thought, while teetering on
the edge is mixed with terror
and wonder, but who will know?
And maybe there was an edge
which over time became the curve
we know today. We grow,
and maybe the earth grows too.

The edge is gone, but still
devours the sanity of all who go
in search of it. Just ask
the ghosts of Martin Luther King, Jr.
or Ghandi at his spinning wheel
to tell of the moment when
the assassin's hand pulled
the curtain down and hope
that men could transcend
their humanness bled and died.

My own explorations scare
me when I lie awake at night
and realize how far we go

to know we aren't alone.
To be a part of something more
we all would follow any lunatic
who made us more than incomplete.

## BIO-WARFARE

The field is fallow,
The weeds in ranks march against the house,
The rose bushes abreast the fence
Are cohorts to the weeds.
The apple tree out back
Looks weary.
The barn, a heap of well-used lumber,
Gives hint that time has passed,
That someone lived here once, but that was in the past.

Now the woods are massing troops, and
By patient biological warfare
The farm becomes a forest.

## AVERTING DEATH BY CHANCE

Like seconds ticking by
upon an aging clock face on the wall
these pines and firs accumulate the past
in piles of browning needles thrown down
to let the future pass.

A gypsy moth staggers by,
on wings that seem to favor chance,
in search of just the proper niche
to incubate her brood.

A winter wren gives chase
and grabs the moth
transforming life to death and back again
before the forest has the chance
to feel the icy larval breath.

## BALANCE

The sky has licked the moon
a couple inches out of round
but still it quiets stars half the sky away.
Trees are gray in thought
their many-fingered limbs groping out,
casting shadows black on gray.
A field of dying grass transformed to mounds of wool,
a lake, a flask to clone the moon within its uterine depths;
these lunar rays reconstitute reality,
compressing depth to linearity,
from color, monochrome,
revealing subtleties lost in day
requiring just the proper balance
of light and dark.

## Awaiting Resurrection

All still and silent, side by side, we sleep
awaiting day to peel away the sands
of darkness carefully packed around our deep
forgetfulness of time and light. Our hands
would touch with recognition if our brains
were more aware; proximity is not
enough to mix two kinds of clay, the grains
retain their aggregate against the night
until the first graying rays release
the stagnant sky, awaken dormant birds
to pluck our bony inner ears and tease
our dreams with something almost given words.
Our eyes open, signals reach our hands,
our lives begin again in day-lit lands.

## COMPOSED BY RAIN

Like typewriter keys bouncing off the platen
the rain plays percussion with my metal roof,
resting now and then to catch his breath.
The words keep dropping from the trees,
letter by letter,
assembled into sentences
they gather weight and volume,
filling pages, then a book,
they slither off
to puddle on the ground.
At times, to make a point
the oak flings an exclamation mark
which later germinates
to show the strength of words
when flung decisively.

## FORGET THE TRUTH

Forget the truth—that scattered bag
of bones and miscellany we all hope
to pile in one convenient place—
and live your life consuming all the scraps
that orbit 'round your slowly spinning soul.
Gather diamonds from the troubled top
of every lake and then return them,
a constant semaphore
to every passing seeker of truth;
harvest gold from every wind
caressed autumn tree before
the ground below has its way
and pulls the pages down
to slowly, coldly burn them up.

## CINEMATIC FLIGHT

A little blood,
a little kicking, hitting, falling down,
a little chase by car or foot,
explosions big and small,
and bullets swarming, plunking, hitting home,
adrenaline pumping,
while muscles tense for flight.
Nowhere to go but sit
and let it drain me dry
of nights alone
and hours spent with strangers.
No need before these scenes
to analyze, to feel, to wonder why,
to feel alone and lonely;
the story sucks me in, sucks me dry,
removes the darker parts of being me,
of being anybody,
sitting there as if I don't exist,
suspended until the lights come on.

CONVERGENCE

Sometimes
I am interrupted in life
To stand at the window
At the precise moment
When day and night
Shake hands—
The colors,
Blue, purple, and red
In infinite shades.
It is then I know the genius
Of Monet,
His obsession with light
And dark and a lonely haystack,
A lifetime of experience
Suspended in that moment
Caught between light and dark.
Somehow it's stark (or is it rich)
Simplicity, more profound
Than books or whole libraries,
Because words cannot describe,
Even pictures only hint.
To see and know
You must be there
At the precise moment in time
When thought and color,
Day and night,
Imperceptibly converge.

## On Hearing the Shanghai Quartet Play Hovhaness

Four pieces of wood and gut
become a forest of strings,
and in between the slanting lines
I hear a bird remembering light
an hour before the dawn.
I search the thicker groves
and hope to see him there,
but as the day explodes
and shadows shorten
the bird escapes
and leaves behind a tree top breeze
that splits the light to fragments
dancing on the leafy floor.
The litter soon dissolves,
revealing orange, red, and white—
scales in motion—
suspended in a rock-lined,
liquid-crystal bowl,
and falling from above—
a cherry tree in bloom—
petals form continents and islands
soon to be destroyed,
sinking piece by piece
to line the ocean floor.
I dive among the fish
and swim down,
down where light is lost
and silence is reality.

YOU ARE MY OVAL
*for JN*

You are my oval, let me sway your count—
the list is long with me, and may it grow
beyond my own circumference and mount
to more. May shapeliness begin to flow
in multi-colored forms from red through blue
that will not fade, no matter what the past
by devious means may resurrect from you
or me to scare the light to leave so fast.

I hold your everything within my breast
and even in the dark a piece of you
illuminates my night, allowing rest
to overtake my fractured points of view—
you fuse my trinity, my east and west,
to singleness and leave me ably blessed.

## POISON OAK

The skin across
the crook of my elbow
is glowing red,
my body convinced
it's found an enemy
to fight.
Histamines recruit
a host of battle drones;
the itch begins.

Retracing steps
the last few days
I can't recall a brush
with leaves of three,
but proof is painted red
across my skin
and nerves,

but evidence
is not a soloist
for truth.
No matter what
the premises
their weight is all
the same at fall's approach,
like leaves burned red
by summer's blast.

Each night our cat
nestles next
to me, snoring quietly,
his body draped
across my arm,
fatigued from
forest jaunts

in search
of rodent prey,
and while I sleep
his day rubs off
on me.

## LEAKY ROOF

The rain, my friend since childhood,
has changed my view this week
as inch by inch it fell
and worked its way within
some hidden crevices
I thought were so well-sealed.

Nothing like a steady
drip to fill a pan
to near capacity.
While sitting on the roof
to patch a phantom hole
the rain runs down my back

and fills another space.
No matter how secure
I made my roof before
the rain still finds a way
to wriggle through my roof
and wrinkle up my skin.

ALPINE NOCTURNE
*Round Valley, near Peter Grub Cabin*

My only fire the stars,
I warm myself on light-years of stellar heat.

Across the alpine meadow silence hugs itself to keep awake
And not a crackling from those distant fires distracts the
     night.

PACIFIC VOYAGE
*for JS*

You float so quietly on your pacific ocean,
your skin so warm to touch, but O so out of touch.
The tubes and wires attached to every body part

are rigging, sails, to catch the gentle wind that draws
your quiet weightless form beyond our skill to reach.
Our hands support you in this blind setting off

to ocean deserts none will ever see the same,
and other hands, invisible and infinite
control the lines and rudder, while you, with steady breath

are sleeping patiently below, content to sleep
or waken. The pilot knows the time and place
to rouse you from your peacefulness, but we who watch

from shore would sail you to a different port, or rush
you back to any point of land, just to touch
your warmth and know you sense us there beside your berth.

MEMORIES OF WIND

Miles of grass caress the passing wind,
a soft answer turned aside and bent
in passing never fully past,
as one long wave it crests but never breaks
and in my car I feel and hear
this surging tide of molecules.

At Grandma West's in Bellingham it seemed more still.
My sister and I would play outside
in grass head high from the knee.
We made our homes of grass
with slightly swaying walls (or still)
and trampled roads between.

Oliver lived there too,
his body 60 or so, his mind barely 12,
(the brother I never had)
we played. Armed for war we walked to the creek,
always smooth as polished wax
just short of where it ducked beneath the road
until our bombs were launched at water skippers.
I don't remember wind in the trees
and the water was only cratered and folded
by Oliver and me at play.

Later in the house we'd use the stereopticon.
Pictures of buildings, mountains,
people I didn't know looked almost real
while Oliver wound the gramophone and played a favorite
    hymn
to the silent wind never rising against the windows of the
    house.

TURNABOUT

The grass, a knife
as strong as tempered steel
divides the wind. Awakened, it
in turn, divides the grass.

WHITE-CROWNED SPARROW

The ocean gave itself wings when you
were born and sang those first descending notes
of praise for frothy wash and wind-blown sand
released reluctantly from probing sea grass roots;

for openness, the undulating hills
beyond the sloping, sandy beach—swept clean
of history with each devouring wave—
forever playing games of chance with wind between

successive ocean storms; for life and death
so entwined, feeding themselves side by side
(as clouds of fertile urchin eggs begin
and end their random lives) the two confide.

Before today my summer desert slept,
my feeder full of other birds. Today
the ocean's breath has spoken through your song
and winter's cooling mists have come to stay.

A REASON TO HOLD YOUR BREATH

You may glory in the possibility
that Moses, Aristotle, Augustine and you
have all shared the same restless air,
that even the same atoms have passed
the lips of each, but by equal chance
these ripening tomatoes on my window sill
have passed the lips of Socrates
as poison brewed to make the truth
more palatable, or that Jesus nearly passed
them through His lips, except He knew
the danger of holding on too long.

What makes me fear to take another breath
is knowledge that we all have breathed
and just enough have breathed beyond
their share. I fear that once
released, re-breathed, these molecules might
again reconstruct the blackest night.

BURIAL BY SKY

As if they fear the sky will fall
today hemlocks, firs and pines
bend low with snow.
The sky stoops too in gray semi-tones
expecting gravity to mediate
between the thirsts of ground and sky.
As the first silent flakes of snow
escape ground-ward, ground and sky
dissolve their great divorce
in white infinity
covering yesterday's drop cloth with a new.

With monochromatic skill the sky gently falls
devoid of malcontent it merely hopes to hide
the penetrating greens and browns
beneath the gray dome of day.
Deceit, subtly woven lies,
belief that visibility confuses truth
support the unity of loss by burial.

LIFE IN THE ATTIC
(After the play *The Diary of Anne Frank*)

Rehearse and re-rehearse the lives
lived out in hidden rooms and closets,
the fear of hiding out,
the fear of being caught,
the endless waiting for food and news,
our lives entwined with theirs
as if we too were trapped
within their skins,
our stomachs tight from lack of food,
our nerves stretched beyond their tensile strength.
We can only guess the pain,
the sense of roots pulled violently from earth
removed from years of pleasant growth
and left to dry and crack in the full sun
of ugly reality, of men turned beasts
who hunt like packs of starving wolves
and feed upon the blood of innocents.
We stop our lives to learn these lines,
to even (if possible) live these lines,
to spend sleepless nights in fear
that we can never understand,
never recreate their lives complete,
only shadows, we walk the stage in safety,
insulated by more than 50 years
and several layers of skin.

LEVELING

Scattered to the compass points
these captured flakes of light
fall, so silently, so lightly,
their weight so inconsequential
they land uninjured to
the ground, geometries en masse
transformed to gentle curve,
the many pointed grass turned dull.

RELUCTANCE

Wind-picked pages of spring and summer
were rifled today,
unpiled and piled and unpiled again.
Some were caught against fences
and weeds detained a few
for lengthy interrogation.
Trees behind my house
budget leaf-drop
reluctant to lose
such carefully crafted manuscripts
no matter how browned the pages.

PREPARATION

An ocean of grass divided by
a river's liquid line,
traced in willow, olive, oak, and eucalyptus,
has drunk its fill at winter's breast
preparing for the drying time.

A red-tailed hawk beyond the river floats—
a swimmer on the land's exhaled breath—
searching for darker specks against the green.
Among some cat tails, screened by trees,
a male red-winged blackbird
recites his mating mantra
and builds his speckled harem.

A committee of woodpeckers
argues beside the river,
and by the nearer trees
another sentences last year's acorns
to the casket of a barren snag.

IN THE BEGINNING

One hundred billion galaxies,
in each, one hundred billion stars,
and no one knows the source
of all this shining mass of hydrogen.

The ancient Greeks,
believing earth was solid ground
saw spheres in motion in the dome above,
with stars attached and moved
by unseen hands of Gods, or nothing but
an unknown initial cause
that set them spinning frictionless
an infinity of years ago.

Today the physics-trained astronomers
look through their telescopes
or scan the sky with radar dish
detecting light in all its varied forms
with all the colors shifted red,
their sparks flung free from birth
of time and space, the twins
whose intertwining tentacles
define the space we're in, begun
in randomness in one mad rush.

Before the Greeks
the Hebrew prophets spoke of words
whose power formed the earth and heavens all
within a week of days and nights,
the speaker, apart from time and space,
alone, the One, I Am, the primal cause,
with no beginning, started all,

and yet, the mysteries remain,
beginning with my own, and all
are gently, firmly held within this curve
of time and space, beginning without end.

## A WHEELCHAIR, NEW ORLEANS, POST-KATRINA

Alone, a wheelchair,
outside the entrance doors,
is silent. Seated there
a man or woman, hard
to know precisely when
a blanket hides the face
and just a bare left arm
and half an ankle are
exposed. It sits, i.e.
the wheelchair, and
holds the lifeless body like
a mother too distraught
to lay her baby down.

DARFUR

Death extends her tresses
auburn-dyed with blood from innocents
resting in the arms of mothers
frozen-faced and hopeless,
ululating dirges for the dying,
readying themselves for the long night.

Dante, Kafka, Bosch attempted
art that only hinted at the torture
raging through these fields of
flesh left baking in the dusty
underside of human nonchalance.
Riding in our air conditioned

domes of steel and glass we pass houses
almost rich enough to feed whole masses
rummaging among the corpses
for anything of value
under the sun, the same
relentless, burning sun.

## BIT PIECE

After years of calloused use
I stretch my metaphor tonight
between the crowded solar spaces
attempting something close enough
to truth to pass for it,
or maybe more—at least to add
a star or two to fill
these empty spaces.

## KAFKA ON THE BEACH

> Gregor pushed himself slowly towards the door, with the help of the easy chair, let go of it there, threw himself against the door, held himself upright against it—the balls of his tiny limbs had a little sticky stuff on them—and rested there momentarily from his exertion.—Franz Kafka, *The Metamorphosis*

I'm an arthropod with two
legs crossed, six at rest, and two
to pen these lines. My eyes
on stalks survey the bouldered plain
for carcasses to plunder,
all the while keeping watch
for gull or peep whose beak
might penetrate to flesh.
The water, never far, provides
a banquet washed
and grilled beneath the sun,
and moistens spiracles
whose capillaries pump
extracted oxygen to keep
my slowly burning fire alive.

## DEGREES OF HARDNESS

The strength of solids is only by degree
as seen by observation over years of soft
against hard (a soft answer turns away wrath),
the hardest rock may seem to split the waves
apart withstanding tons of force unchanged,
apparently, and yet a year from now if I
reseat myself above this continental edge
the oystercatchers will be using a fraction less
than searched today for dinner, kelp
will find new surfaces to hold itself in place,
the splash-zone algae will have stained
another layer of the past, and yet
my feet seem little different in
relation to the edge. It's not as if
the continent has lost—the ocean gained—
but water's dull, relentless edge has cut
a softer place on which to pile itself
ahead of storm-waves generated miles
away, the prize of patience, quietly
at work with words too soft
to waken fear or stubbornness.

## JOSHUA STOOD STILL

> *Then spake Joshua to the LORD in the day when the LORD delivered up the Amorites before the children of Israel, and he said in the sight of Israel, Sun, stand thou still upon Gibeon; and thou, Moon, in the valley of Ajalon. And the sun stood still, and the moon stayed, until the people had avenged themselves upon their enemies. Is not this written in the book of Jasher? So the sun stood still in the midst of heaven, and hasted not to go down about a whole day. (Joshua 10:12-13)*

When Joshua made the sun stand still
what proof was needed to support
the longer length of day made light
for killing? Warriors that day

were proof enough—as stabbing,
slashing, bleeding each expired
in his own way—of what? The sun
indeed appeared to hover long

and long the incorrect opinion held
its power over church and state
until presumptuous Galileo moved
the sun and spun the earth.

Time is still at center stage,
though relative to space we now
know every change in space
has gravity enough to spare.

*REDUCTIO AD ABSURDUM*

A Benedictine monk a thousand years ago,
alone, reciting texts—strings of words
as mantras warding off the demons of
the night—and passing beads between
his fingers as he cants the virgin's praises,
little knows the use his cell will have
in hands that later hold a tiny glass
to view the honeycombed bark
of cork oak, invoking recognition of
identical and sparsely furnished cells.

Though dead, the cork recounts
a time when cloistered cytoplasm pulsed
with molecules, with rosaries composed
of histone-shrouded DNA caressed by clouds
of fingered proteins, a secret language
spoken silently beneath the range of sight
with letters made of sugars, phosphates, nitrogen,
all bound by lipid walls and protein furnishings.

The manuscript has only now been studied enough
to see the words in all their clarity,
and still the lexicon is incomplete, a mystery
unfolding and yet still deeper after each attempt.
The quietly swaying Talmudic scholar knows
this kind of truth, and Buddha laughs
at such naïveté, that life could be confined
in letters on a page or stored for easy reference
as 1s and 0s in silicon.

BETTER NOT TO KNOW

Between Jerusalem and Jericho the road is dry,
and rocks, collected from the slopes above,
are scattered like the leftover missiles of
a stoning, missing only blood to paint the scene,

and lost among the thistles lies the refuse lost
or thrown away, the empty cruse, the leather strap
that once held a sandal to a foot, a frayed piece
of rope lost in anger at a stubborn ass,

and out of place (and yet familiar) a trail of blood
connects the road with a twitching mass of flesh—
unclothed but for a bloodied loin cloth half askew—
a sort of refuse, more to some than others, left

to slowly die or live in pain. Convenience keeps
the smelly details hazily obscure, as if
by ignorance excuse is given credence, as if
by any ruse the laws of common decency

can lose their force, as if the someone-else-
will-surely-stop defense erases blame.
And so, one by one we pass, anonymous, when all
the time we know we know the bleeding man.

## GENERAL THEORY

> Einstein said that space is curved and that matter is the
> source of the curvature.—*Richard Feynman*

If, as Einstein claimed,
time and space are curved, always,
traveling south becomes tomorrow
traveling north, explaining
why the earth is round(ish):
other shapes are disallowed, little
more than local appearances.

Going small, the bubbles
flying for the top of my diet cola
reach around their precious
packages of $CO_2$ which rupture
with a pop at the skin separating
two realities, and motes swimming
on the lighted air across my kitchen
table, although rough, approximate this
same pervasive bending on themselves.

Light itself, the pure distillation
of perfection's troubled ore, is
not immune to meddling.
Passing massive stars sprinting
straight from A to B is still a
curve in search of some way to
reach back again.

Wind outside my window
travels past each tree, each
leaf, to meet itself once past and

traced across the landscape,
reaching consummation
in returning to the earth its
need to bend all things the same.

## HOW MANY YEARS DID IT TAKE FOR LOT'S WIFE TO MELT?

*But his wife looked back from behind him, and she became a pillar of salt.* (Genesis 19:26)


Baked by years of sun and just enough
rain to harden salt into stone,
carved by wind and shaped by
passing flocks of goats who
lick the crust between their
meals of desert scrub and thorn;
in time a pillar forms after
curve and fold give way to ever
smoother form, a fading into
darkness where the truths we
once perceived so well are
lost among the ever shifting
surface left unchiseled.

Hammer and chisel force these
weathered sediments apart:
fossils are the neurons
of the earth's forgotten thoughts,
memories preserved awaiting
reconstruction, reminding
us that history fades without a
medium, the softest
first to melt and seep away
salt and then the harder
minerals, until all has melted
into stone that sinks under
expectation, memories, half-told
lies that ring of truth when
placed beside a Lucite verdict
in a well-protected museum case.

## 10 Minutes to Live

Fully engage with every atom,
every molecule spinning
through the spaces
in between your pieces.

Hold yourself and others
warmly, feel the pulsing
blood, the radiating
heat in search of rest.

Fill the silence
carefully, or maybe
not at all when wordy
musings hide joyous,

recklessness, where truth is
less the syllable and
more the waiting
for. For what? To

know, past every question
where that far country's
boundaries begin and
end and know with

certainty the truth that's
never shared or
shared with all in
equal knowing.

DEEPER MYSTERIES

Columbus, Eric the Red, Magellan, Vasco de Gama, Cook
and how many more considered the shrinking size
of distance, the ease by which the world closes in
and offers what was once unknown, a well-known track,

a highway, mapped precisely now with GPS. The only ones
who see this three quarter's part of earth so unexceptional
are those who never filter concentrate the specks
that hover in the photic soup their ship's prow is slicing
    through;

who never burrow deep beneath the heaving hills and valleys;
who never hear the silent siren call in darkness hovering
    endlessly
above abyssal plains and trenches where the rain of carbon
    snow
continues falling past the ravening host of microbes eating in

eternal winter; who have never probed the rifts that spew
the smokes of hell (another meal for yet another swarm
encased in blood-red hosts); and never floated half
between the boiling surface and the lonesome benthic calm

where night never ends and many make their own
alchemic glow and predatory eyes collect the faintest glow
of prey; who never see the teeming masses living, dying,
    being born
beneath their swiftly moving crafts intent on voyage end.

A COMPOSITE POEM

The *Centaurea* of the *Cosmos* was,
according to the *Parthenium*, the earth,
believing otherwise was a *Zinnia*,
but now as any *Aster*-onomer will claim,
unless you are *Senecio*, that everyone,
even *Uropappus*, knows beyond a doubt
we *Arnica* even near. Even theologians now
*Layia* side those ancient *Madia* ideas,
but keep on singing *Anthemis* to God,
and the *Eriophyllum* with *Bellis* loud enough
to reach the *Arctium*. *Agoseris* another
explanation *Adenocaulon* yet—
I'm *Bidens* my time until my *Calendula*
is not so full—or so says my wife
except I have not *Aster* yet (she
*Grindelia* to herself, the humor of
it all *Crepis* to her face). *Anthemis*
the sum of explanations unless you'd
*Lactuca* sip *Ambrosia* on *Erigeron*
the coast of *Xanthium*, *Lasthenia* piece
of *Solidago* where *Achillea* met *Antennaria*.

## A SPEECH

Invited here to speak to you
because I once wrote a book
that no one ever reads today.
I hope to seem well-read,

aware of subtle themes that weave
their threads invisibly
except to those like me who are
anointed by the muse.

I try to give away my gift
of higher consciousness, my hand
unconsciously pulling on
my beard, then held aloft

in pseudo-papal blessing, food
for shriveling intellectualists
who burp from stomachs bloated by
the last 100 meals

they feasted on—or should I say
they chewed and swallowed pretentiously,
congratulating emptily
like proper talking heads?

But let me not offend without
some irony to make you smile:
as brave Phidippides I've run
this race for you alone,

to nobly speak eternal truths
designed to purge, like bitter herbs,
the lies we all pretend to hate,
my Hippocratic oath

to do no harm but to myself,
while secretly my epitaph
takes shape, "He ran the Marathon
for us, and then he died."

ALCHEMIC INEQUALITY

The atomic weight of gold (Au) is 197 grams,
while that of lead (Pb) is 207 grams. The irony
is only now apparent looking through the eyes
of alchemy with the brains of modern chemistry.

The years spent in boiling lead and breathing
mercuric fumes, the goal so close, while ignorant of
the vast inequity between two such heavy rocks
so randomly assigned their worth. How many died

so close, they thought, to riches gained by sweat
and secret incantations? How many grains of wheat,
their gold more practical, were lost while fires
of coal and charcoal roasted worthless stones?

I WRITE

I write because my hands do not retract
like tooled robotic arms devoid of sense.

I argue late at night with other parts of me,
colluding with my hands. They all

define reality in slightly different ways,
resisting channels carved by any other body part.

My right hand a fist against the whole,
it slashes out the truth its own relentless way.

www.ingramcontent.com/pod-product-compliance
Lightning Source LLC
Chambersburg PA
CBHW020521030426
42337CB00011B/490